basic
materials
for the
piano student

BROWN

MUSIC SERIES

Edited by FREDERICK W. WESTPHAL, *Ph. D.*
Sacramento State College Sacramento, California

basic
materials
for the
piano student

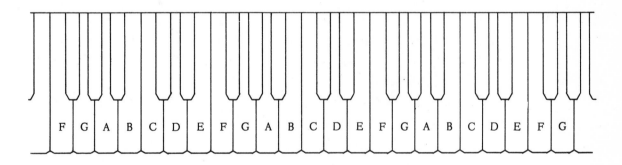

MARCELLE VERNAZZA, Editor

Department of Music

San Francisco State College

San Francisco, California

WM. C. BROWN COMPANY PUBLISHERS

135 SOUTH LOCUST STREET   ●   DUBUQUE, IOWA

Manufactured by WM. C. BROWN CO. INC., Dubuque, Iowa
Printed in U. S. A.

Table of Contents

V

Introduction

This book is an organized collection of information and materials intended for use in presenting the piano as a basic tool for musicians. It is designed for the student who has a special interest in music. It can be used as a text and source book for elementary and intermediate piano classes or studio lessons, as an aid to elementary theory classes, as an enrichment for students studying more than one instrument, as a guide for helping the general music teacher, or as a special study for advanced pianists whose previous instruction has been limited to keyboard literature.

Included is a study guide, which divides the material into a four-term study. In an accelerated study the first and second terms can be combined.

The book includes the following:

1. Scales and Arpeggios
2. Formal Keyboard Harmony
3. Informal Harmonization and Transposition of Melodies
4. Technical Exercises
5. Piano Adaptations of Music of Various Media
6. Songs to Play and Sing
7. List of Recommended Keyboard Literature for Parallel Study
8. Listening Guide for Standard Piano Compositions
9. Study Guide

The scale section includes the traditional major and minor scales as well as chromatic, whole tone, pentatonic, and modal patterns. These are included to broaden the study of scales and to provide a background for the analysis of piano literature. Tonic and dominant seventh arpeggios are also included.

The keyboard harmony section supports and enriches the early traditional theory courses and at the same time adheres to basic pianistic concepts.

The section with melodies to be harmonized and transposed encourages creativity and freedom in improvisation. Basic accompaniment patterns for the harmonization of the songs are an outgrowth of the keyboard harmony exercises. Suggestions for developing appropriate accompaniment patterns are given.

A variety of technical exercises has been included to build good coordination patterns and to cover problems of technique encountered in the early study of the piano.

The section with piano arrangements of music for various media gives the student an opportunity to study at close range many famous compositions otherwise not readily available. Playing these on the keyboard produces greater understanding and appreciation of the compositions and stimulates an interest in hearing them in their original form.

Eleven songs for playing and singing have been arranged in piano style. These arrangements are satisfying but not difficult.

Standard piano selections for listening have been arranged in program groups representing different centuries, styles, and composers. Listening to piano music of this type builds respect for and an understanding of the piano as a concert instrument.

The study guide outlines a four-term course making use of the materials in this book plus supplementary books. However, this text makes no effort to impose any teaching method upon the instructor. The basic materials found here should be presented to fit the needs of the student.

PART I

Scales and Arpeggios

Major and Minor Scales

The major and minor scales have been grouped according to their closest and most common relationships. Each major is presented with its parallel* minor (same tonic) and with its relative minor (same signature). Both relationships are important and should be studied.

A study of major scales and their parallel minors builds a concept of scale intervals and their significance.

A study of major scales and their relative minors builds a concept of signatures and their significance.

*Also called tonic minor.

A Sequential Study of Major and Minor Scales

Study intervals as a preparation for scales. (pages 34-35)

Play all major and minor scales ascending and descending one octave, each hand alone. (pages 4 to 11) Learn all key signatures as you study scales. (page 3)

Play all major and minor scales ascending and descending one octave, hands together.

Play all major and minor scales ascending and descending two octaves, each hand alone.

Play all major and minor scales ascending and descending two octaves, hands together.

Play all major and minor scales ascending and descending three and four octaves, hands together.

Play in rhythms. (page 12)

Harmonize all major and minor scales. (page 14)

The Key Circle

A Study of Keys and Their Signatures

The capital letters on the outside of the circle indicate the major keys.

The small letters on the inside of the circle indicate the relative minor keys.

Moving clockwise around the circle (or moving up by fifths on the keyboard) add a sharp or take away a flat.

Moving counter-clockwise around the circle (or moving up by fourths on the keyboard) add a flat or take away a sharp.

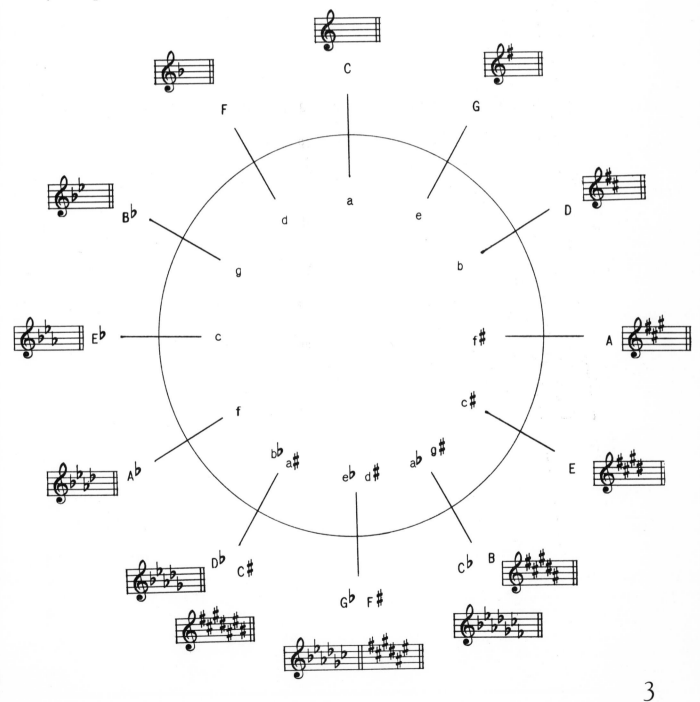

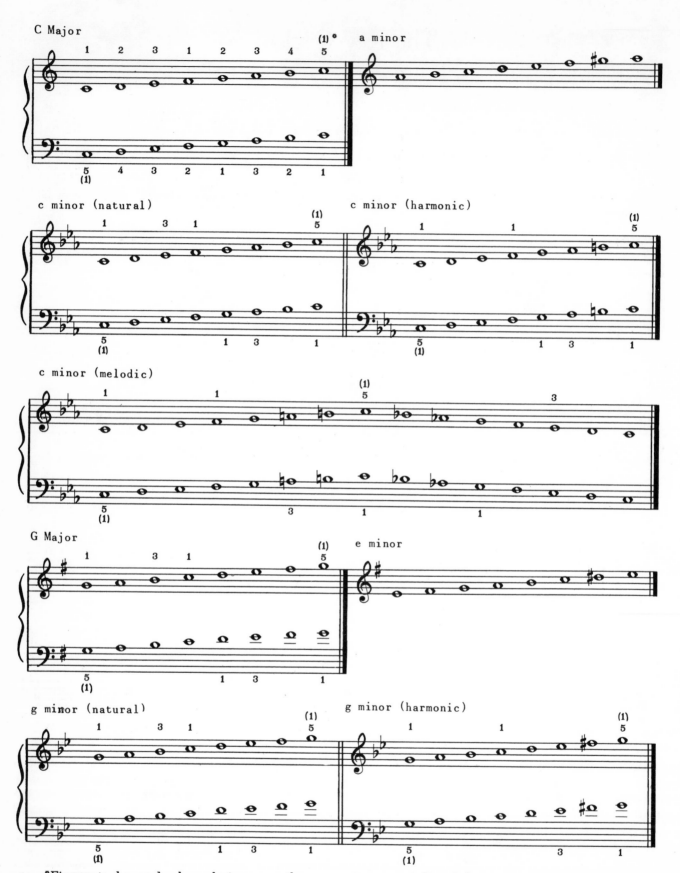

*Fingers to be used when playing more than one octave are indicated by
parentheses.

4

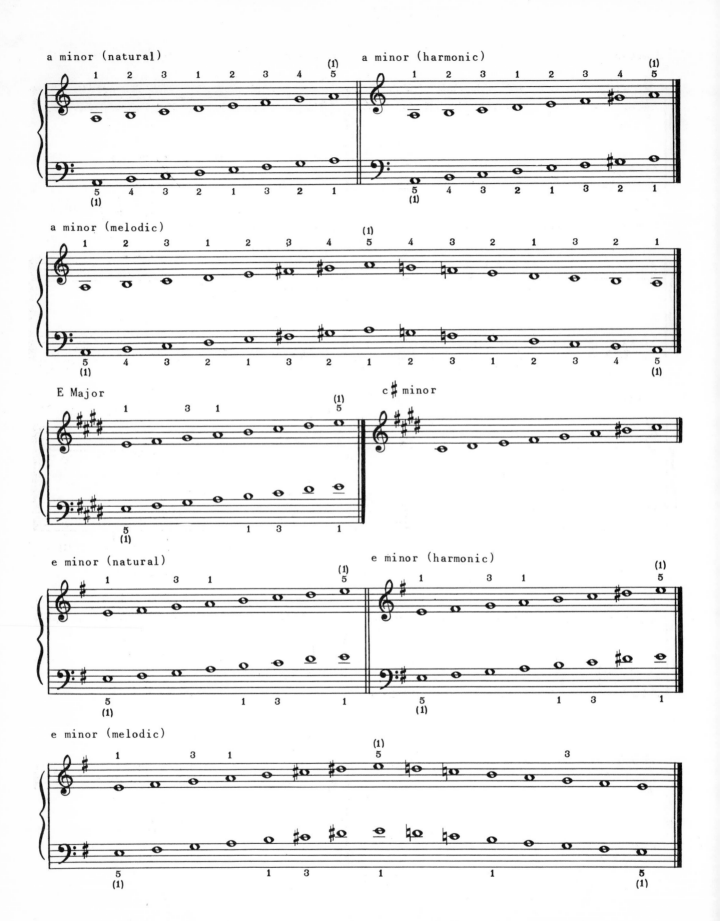

a minor (natural)

a minor (harmonic)

a minor (melodic)

E Major

c♯ minor

e minor (natural)

e minor (harmonic)

e minor (melodic)

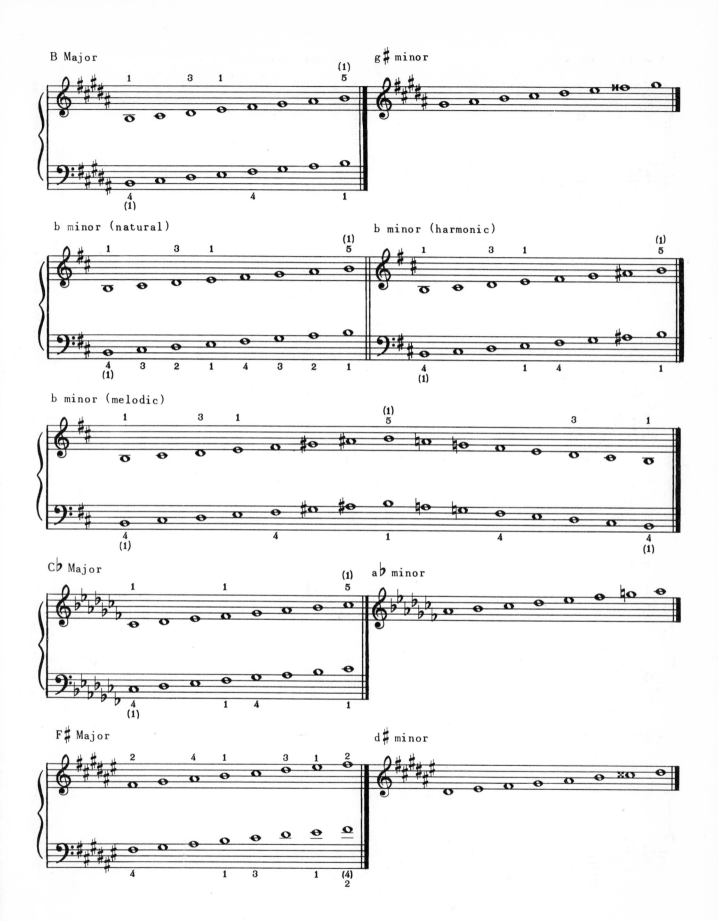

8

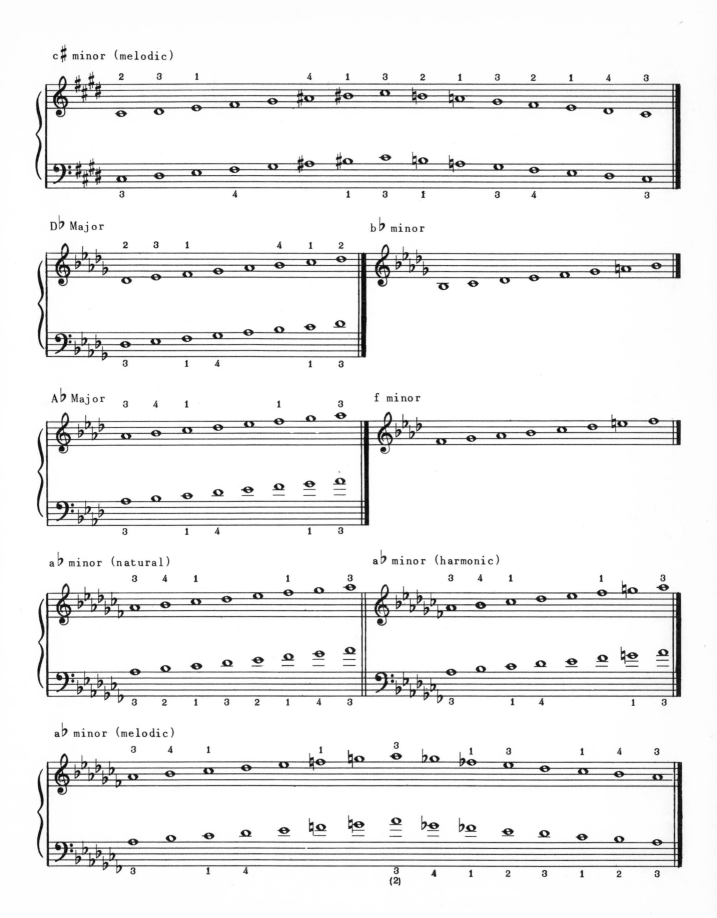

9

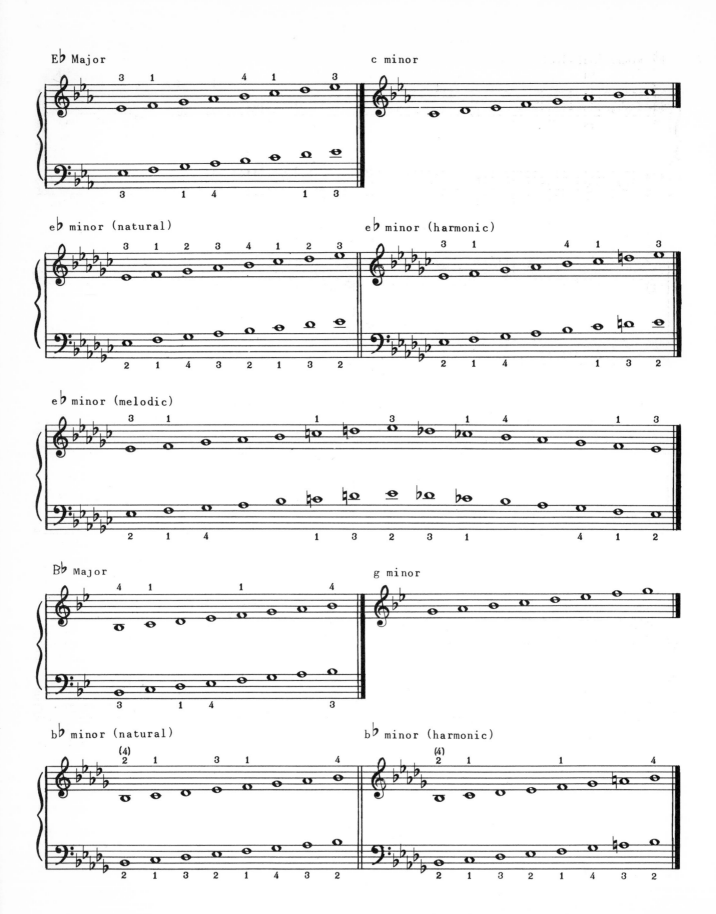

10

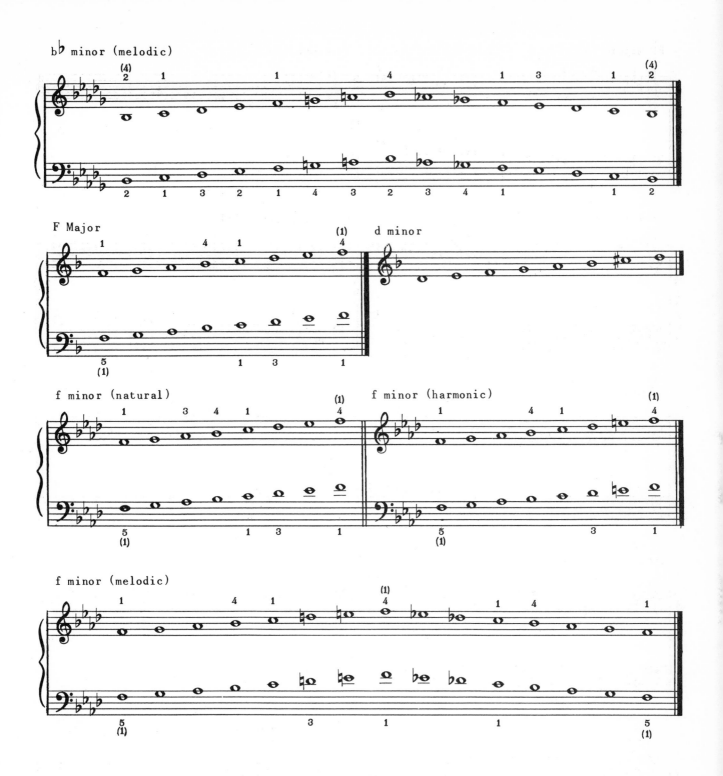

Below is the C major scale in different rhythms. Play all scales using these rhythmic patterns:

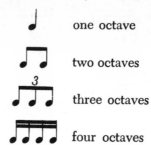

one octave

two octaves

three octaves

four octaves

12

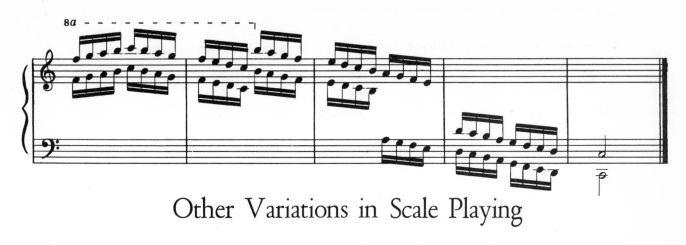

Other Variations in Scale Playing

C Major Scale Descending and Ascending

C Major Scale in Contrary Motion

C Major Scale in Alternating Octaves

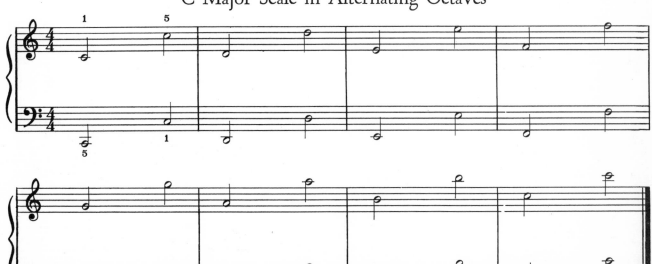

13

C Major Scale Harmonized

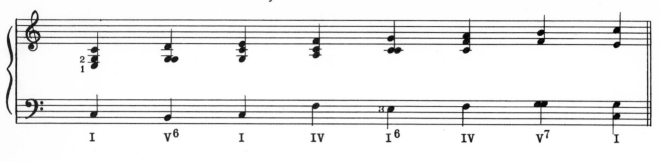

I   V⁶   I   IV   I⁶   IV   V⁷   I

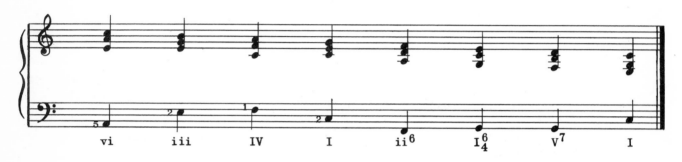

vi   iii   IV   I   ii⁶   I⁶₄   V⁷   I

C Minor Scale Harmonized

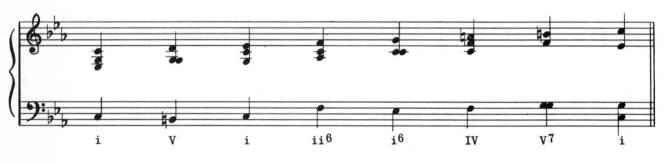

i   V   i   ii⁶   i⁶   IV   V⁷   i

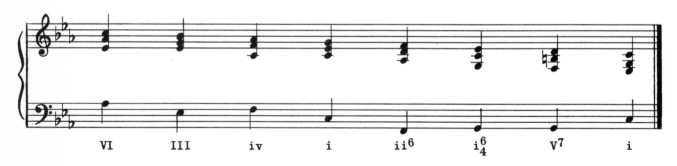

VI   III   iv   i   ii⁶   i⁶₄   V⁷   i

14

A Sequential Study of the Chromatic Scale

Play ascending and descending, one octave, each hand alone. Repeat, hands together.

Play ascending and descending two octaves, hands together. Repeat three, four octaves.

Play from the lowest octave to the highest, increasing speed as you play. Play from the highest to the lowest, increasing speed. Use light surface touch.

Play the following variations:

> in contrary motion
> similar motion, two octaves apart
> in minor thirds (starting l.h. on c♯ — r.h. on e)
> in octaves
> in alternating octaves (see next page)

Find chromatic passages in piano literature.

Two examples are: Für Elise — Ludwig van Beethoven
Premiere Ballade Opus 23 — Frederic Chopin

Chromatic Scale

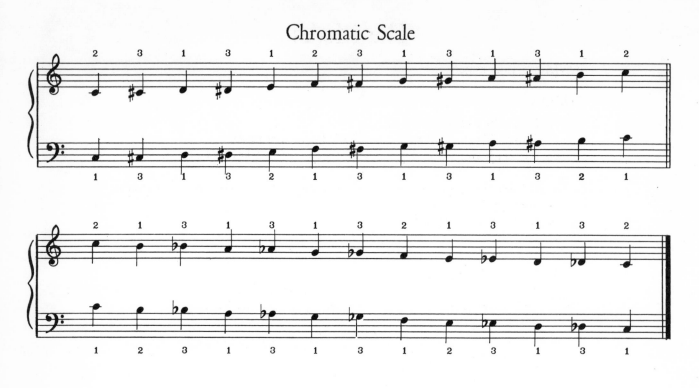

Chromatic Scale in Alternating Octaves (a variation)

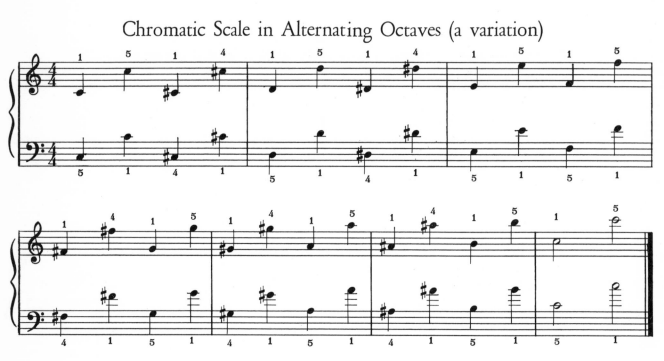

The Modes

IONIAN — Like major.

DORIAN

1. Like 2 to 2 of a major scale.
2. Sounds like natural minor with the 6th degree raised.
3. Its relative major is down a whole step, and it takes that key signature, **or:**
4. It takes the key signature of the tonic minor and appropriate accidentals are supplied.
5. Example: d e f g a b c d

PHRYGIAN

1. Like 3 to 3 of a major scale.
2. Sounds like natural minor with 2nd degree lowered.
3. Its relative major is two whole steps (a major 3rd) lower, and it takes that key signature, or:
4. It takes the key signature of the tonic minor and appropriate accidentals are supplied.
5. Example: e f g a b c d e

LYDIAN

1. Like 4 to 4 of a major scale.
2. Sounds like major with the 4th degree raised.
3. Its relative major is 2 1/2 steps (perfect fourth) lower and it takes that key signature, or:
4. It takes the key signature of the tonic major and appropriate accidentals are supplied.
5. Example: f g a b c d e f

MIXOLYDIAN

1. Like 5 to 5 of a major scale.
2. Sounds like major with the 7th degree lowered.
3. Its relative major is down 3 1/2 steps (perfect fifth), and it takes that key signature, or:
4. It takes the key signature of the tonic major and appropriate accidentals are supplied.
5. Example: g a b c d e f g

AEOLIAN

Like natural minor. Example: a b c d e f g a

LOCRIAN — Like 7 to 7 of a major scale. Example: b c d e f g a b
     Seldom used.

A Sequential Study of the Modes

Play all the modal scales as constructed on white keys (untransposed). (page 19)

Learn their names and memorize their patterns of steps and half steps.

Play all the modes constructed on C as tonic. (See page 17 for other information concerning modes.)

Transpose the modes using C♯ as tonic for each, then D as tonic, and so on through all twelve notes of the chromatic scale. (Locrian may be left out since it is seldom used.)

Pieces using these modes may be found in the *Mikrokosmos* volumes by Béla Bartok. Find and reconstruct the modes found in these pieces.

Modes

(untransposed)

Ionian
(major scale)

Dorian
(2 to 2 of
major scale)

Phrygian
(3 to 3 of
major scale)

Lydian
(4 to 4 of
major scale)

Mixolydian
(5 to 5 of
major scale)

Aeolian
(6 to 6 of
major scale)
(natural minor)

Locrian
(7 to 7 of
major scale)

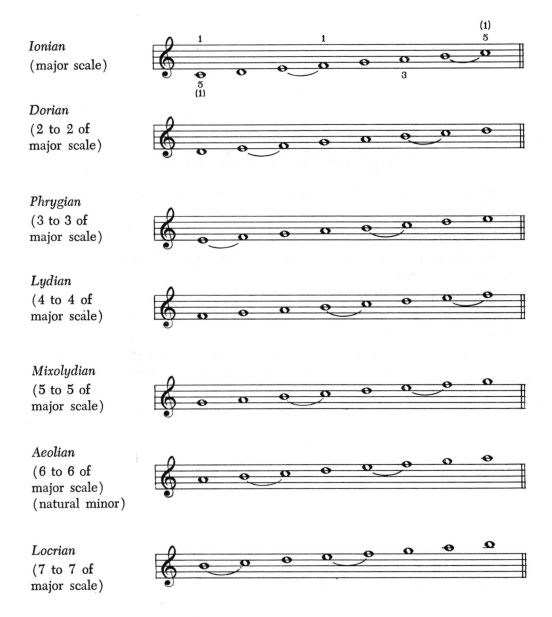

Modal Scales Constructed on C as Tonic

Ionian (same as C major))

Dorian using the signature of the relative major (B♭)

Dorian using the signature of the parallel minor (c)

Phrygian using the signature of the relative major (A♭)

Phrygian using the signature of the parallel minor (c)

Lydian using the signature of the relative major (G)   G)

Lydian using the signature of the parallel major (C)

Mixolydian using the signature of the relative major (F)

Mixolydian using the signature of the parallel major (C)

Aeolian using the signature of the relative major (E♭)

The Pentatonic Scale

An Introductory Study of the Five Tone Scale (1-2-3-5-6)

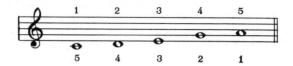

It is sometimes called the black note scale because it can be played on the black notes of the piano.

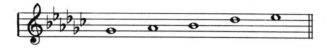

Pentatonic melodies are found in the folk music of many countries as well as in the works of famous composers. All of these have individual characteristics and variations.

Three contrasting treatments of the pentatonic scale are to be found in (1) Prelude II, "Voiles" Ier livre — Claude Debussy (2) Volumes 2 and 3, Mikrokosmos — Béla Bartok (3) *Auld Lang Syne* — a Scotch air (page 70).

Traditional harmonization of pentatonic melodies, such as Auld Lang Syne, destroys the pentatonic feeling by adding the other tones of the scale.

Swing Low Sweet Chariot (page 134) and *Old Brass Wagon* (page 65) are examples of other types of pentatonic melodies.

Sequential Study of the Pentatonic Scale

1. Play as illustrated, each hand alone, then hands together.
2. Play in every key. (Leave out 4 and 7 of the major scale or 2 and 6 of the natural minor.)
3. Analyse the scale as found in the above examples. Find other examples in piano and folk music.
4. Interesting melodic patterns with accompaniments can be improvised entirely within the pentatonic scale.

Improvise a sixteen measure piece on the pentatonic scale using the A (four measures), B (eight measures), A (four measures). For other suggestions see lesson on damper pedal.

The Whole Tone Scale

The whole tone scale is exactly what the name implies — a scale with a whole step between each member of the scale.   It can be built starting on any note.

The following examples give two possible fingerings.

Using the first example, build the scale on C, D, E, F♯, G♯, or A♯.

Using the second example, build the scale on F, G, A, B, C♯, or D♯.

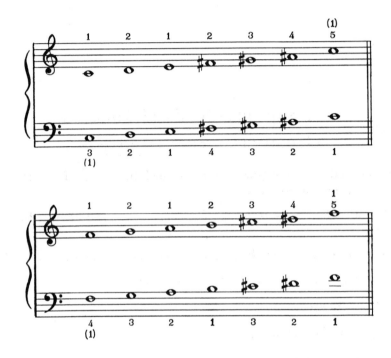

Composers of tonal impressionistic music used this scale extensively.   Some examples to examine are:

(1) Prelude II, "Voiles," Ier livre — Claude Debussy
(2) Jeux d'Eau — Maurice Ravel

Improvisation on the Whole Tone Scale

Interesting scale and arpeggio-like passages can be improvised on the whole tone scale.   When improvising, experiment with the damper and sostenuto pedals.   (See pages 82 and 83.)

A Sequential Study of Tonic and Dominant Seventh Arpeggios

(The study of arpeggios should parallel the study of major and minor scales and chord inversions.)

Play as a block chord, noting fingering, each hand alone. Repeat hands together.

Play one octave, each hand alone, then hands together.

Play two octaves, three octaves, four octaves.

Play in rhythms.

Play with the following variations:

    with staccato touch

    in octaves

    in contrary motion

    combining two positions, one in each hand

Tonic Arpeggios

*Fingers to be used when playing more than one octave are indicated in parenthesis.

26

27

28

Dominant Seventh Arpeggios

30

PART II

Keyboard Harmony Exercises

The keyboard harmony exercises in this book parallel the formal study of elementary harmony. The emphasis here is on keyboard activities leading to the understanding of the theory of harmony. The ability to play the exercises in every key is essential to a successful culmination of the study. Directions for study and practice are given for each exercise. The exercises are a complete study by themselves, but may also be used as a supplementary text with any traditional harmony text.

The three voice, bass clef progressions are included to correlate common accompaniment patterns with the traditional four-part harmony. They will also be useful when harmonizing and transposing the melodies found in Part III. In Part III direct reference is made to these patterns when they are appropriate for the harmonization of songs.

Keyboard Harmony

Intervals

An interval is the distance between two tones.

Intervals are classified according to the number of degrees they encompass, including both the top and the bottom.

1. *Practice* locating and playing these intervals, starting on any tone.

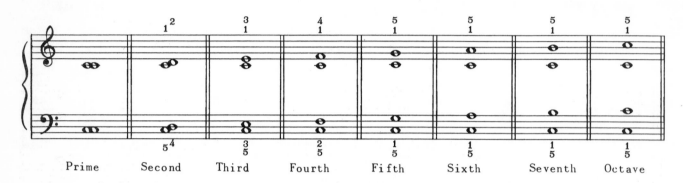

Prime　　Second　　Third　　Fourth　　Fifth　　Sixth　　Seventh　　Octave

Kinds of Intervals

Practice locating and playing these intervals, starting on any tone.

2. *Major Interval*:　Upper tone found in the major scale of the lower tone.

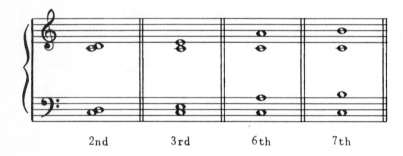

2nd　　3rd　　6th　　7th

3. *Perfect Interval*:　Either tone found in the major scale of the other tone.

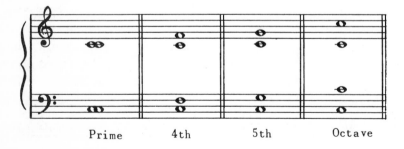

Prime　　4th　　5th　　Octave

4. *Minor Interval*: One half step smaller than a major interval.

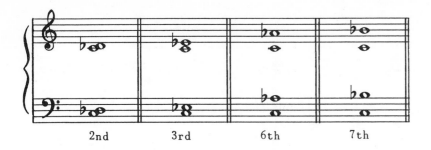

2nd   3rd   6th   7th

5. *Diminished Interval*: One half step smaller than perfect and minor interval.

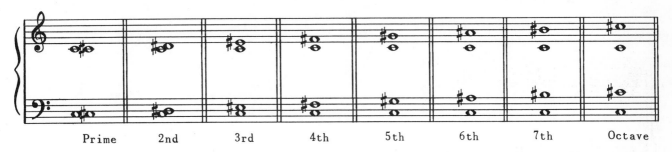

2nd   3rd   4th   5th   6th   7th   Octave

6. *Augmented Interval*: One half step larger than perfect and major intervals.

Prime   2nd   3rd   4th   5th   6th   7th   Octave

Triads

A triad is a chord of three tones; a fundamental tone with a third and fifth.

Triads are classified as: major, minor, diminished, and augmented.

7. *Practice* building these triads on other tones.

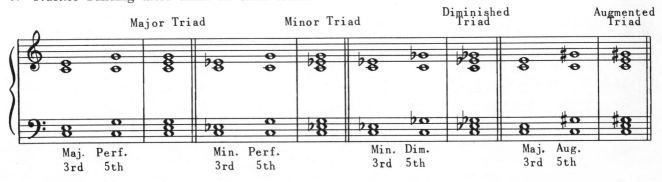

Major Triad   Minor Triad   Diminished Triad   Augmented Triad

Maj. Perf.   Min. Perf.   Min. Dim.   Maj. Aug.
3rd 5th   3rd 5th   3rd 5th   3rd 5th

8. *Diatonnotic triads* (on scale tone).

Only scale tones are used. In minor use the harmonic form.

Practice building these triads as you study each scale.

C: I   ii   iii   IV   V   vi   vii°   I

c: i   ii°   III⁺   iv   V   VI   vii°   i

9. Locate and play the I (tonic) triad in every major and minor key.

C: I   c: i

10. Locate and play the first and fifth tones of every scale.

11. Locate and play the I and V (dominant) triads in every key.

12. Locate and play the first and fourth tones of every scale.

13. Locate and play the I and IV (sub-dominant) triads in every key.

14. Triads in a broken chord pattern

Play every major and minor triad using this arrangement.

37

15. Triad Inversions.

Invert every major and minor triad.

16. Variations of Major and Minor Triad Inversions

Practice these on all major and minor triads.

Continue these variations to the top of the keyboard and down.

38

17. I IV I — Close Position — root, third, fifth in soprano.

Play in every key.

18. I IV I — Three Voices — Bass clef.

Play in every key.

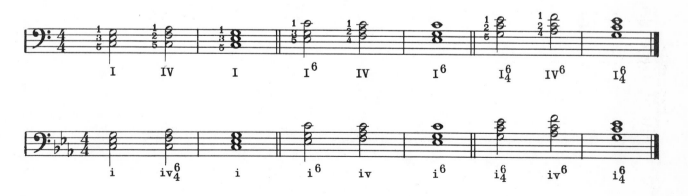

I   IV   I   I^6 IV   I^6 I$^6_4$ IV^6 I$^6_4$

i   iv$^6_4$ i   i^6 iv   i^6 i$^6_4$ iv^6 i$^6_4$

19. I V I — Close Position (soprano, alto, tenor within one octave).

Root, third, fifth in soprano.

Play in every key.

20. I V I — Three voices — Bass clef

Play in every key.

21. I IV V I — Close Position — root, third, fifth in soprano

Play in every key.

22. I IV V I — Three Voices — Bass clef.

Play in every key.

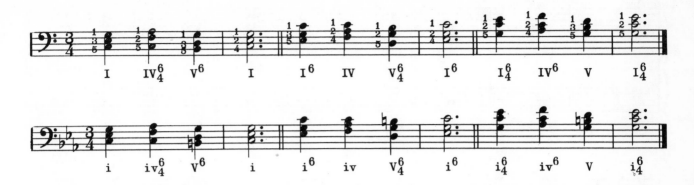

The Seventh Chord is a chord of four tones. It is made by adding a third to the top of a triad (a seventh from the root of the chord).

23. The V7 or Dominant 7 (complete and incomplete).

Play in every key.

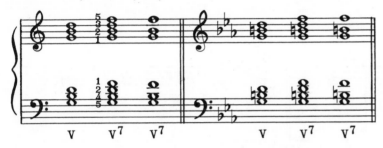

24. Inversion of the Dominant Seventh Chord.

Play these inversions in every key.

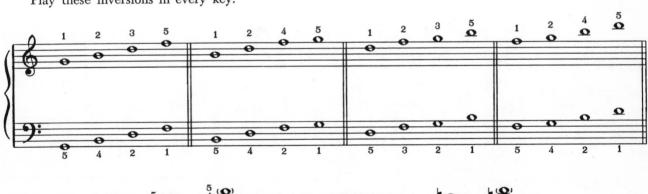

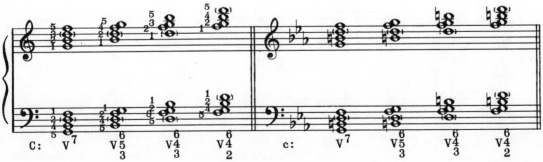

25. I V7 I, i V7 i

Play in every key.

26. I V$_5^6$ I, i V$_5^6$ i

Play in every key.

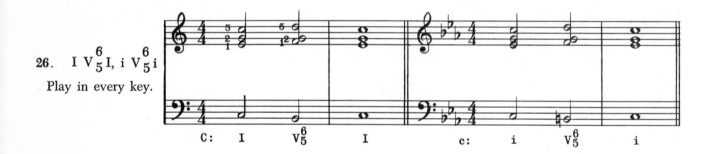

C: I   V$_5^6$ I   c: i   V$_5^6$ i

27. I V$_3^4$ I, i V$_3^4$ i

Play in every key.

C: I   V$_3^4$ I   c: i   V$_3^4$ i

28. I V$_2^4$ I, i V$_2^4$ i

Play in every key.

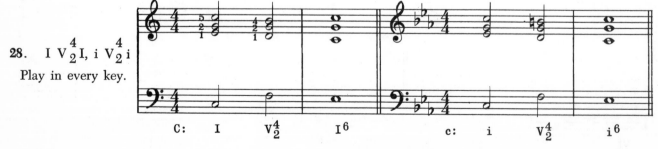

C: I   V$_2^4$ I^6 c: i   V$_2^4$ i^6

29. I V$^6_5$ I, i V$^6_5$ i — Three voices — Bass clef

Play in every key.

30. I V$^4_3$ I, i V$^4_3$ i — Three voices — Bass clef

Play in every key.

31. I V$^4_2$ I, i V$^4_2$ i — Three voices — Bass clef

Play in every key.

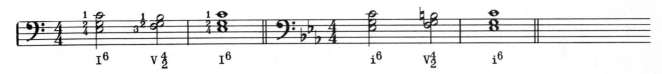

32. I IV V7 I, i iv V7 i

Play in every key.

33. I IV V7 I, i iv V7 i — Three voices — Bass clef

34. A chord progression with a waltz bass.

Play in every key.

Improvisation on a chord progression.

Play the bass as written.

Create a melody above it.

44

35.   I ii^6 I $\frac{6}{4}$ V I

Play in every major key.

36.   i ii6 i$\frac{6}{4}$ V i

Play in every minor key.

37.

C: I   IV$\frac{6}{4}$ ii   V$\frac{6}{5}$ I

38.   Neopolitan Sixth (with and without the I$\frac{6}{4}$)

Play in every minor key.

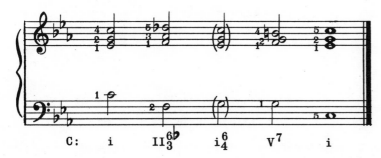

C: i   II$\frac{6\flat}{3}$ i$\frac{6}{4}$ V^7 i

45

39. Secondary Sevenths (diatonic)

Play in every major key.

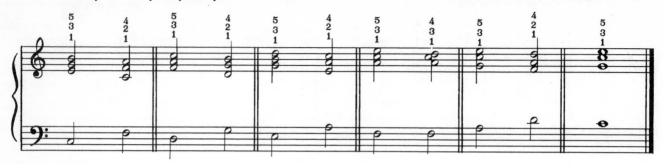

40. Sevenths, ninths, elevenths, thirteenths.

Play in every major key.

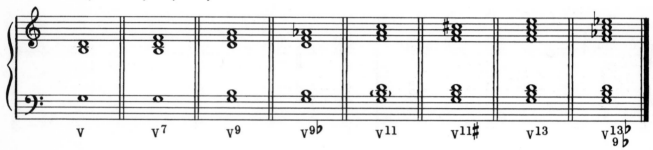

V   V⁷   V⁹   V⁹♭   V¹¹   V¹¹♯   V¹³   V¹³♭⁹♭

Secondary Dominants

41. V7 of V (Major Mode)

Play in every major key.

I   V⁷ of V   V   V⁷   I

42. V7 of ii (Major Mode)

Play in every major key.

I   V⁷ of ii   ii   V⁷   I

43.   V7 of vi (Major Mode)

Play in every major key.

44.   V7 of IV (Major Mode)

Play in every major key.

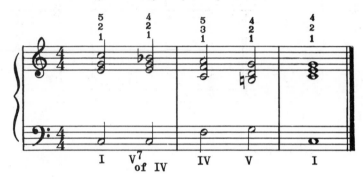

45.   V7 of iii (Major Mode)

Play in every major key.

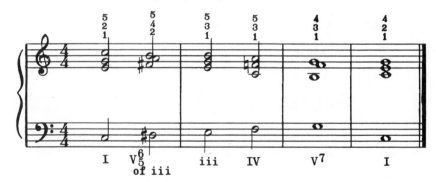

46.   Three Voices — Bass clef

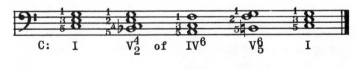

47.

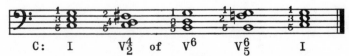

47

48.

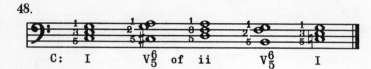

C: I V_5^6 of ii V_5^6 I

49.

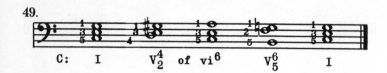

C: I V_2^4 of vi^6 V_5^6 I

50.

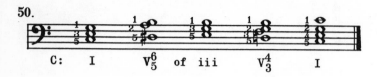

C: I V_5^6 of iii V_3^4 I

51.

c: i V_5^6 of III   iv V_5^6 I

52.

c: i^6 V_5^6 of III V_5^6 of Nea. ♭II V_5^6 i

53.

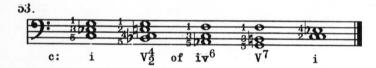

c: i V_2^4 of iv^6 V^7 i

54.

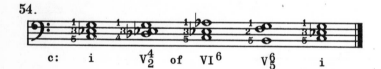

c: i V_2^4 of VI^6 V_5^6 i

Modulation

Secondary dominants may be used to modulate from one key to another.

Example: V of V to the dominant key
          V of ii to super-tonic key
          V of vi to sub-mediant key
          V of IV to sub-dominant key
          V of iii to mediant

A pivot chord is the chord common to both the original key and the one to which you are modulating. It is this chord that links the two keys. After reaching the pivot chord, establish the new key by remaining in it.

Melodic Fragments and chord progressions for improvisation.

Chord Progressions with a rhythm pattern.

Create a melody for the right hand.

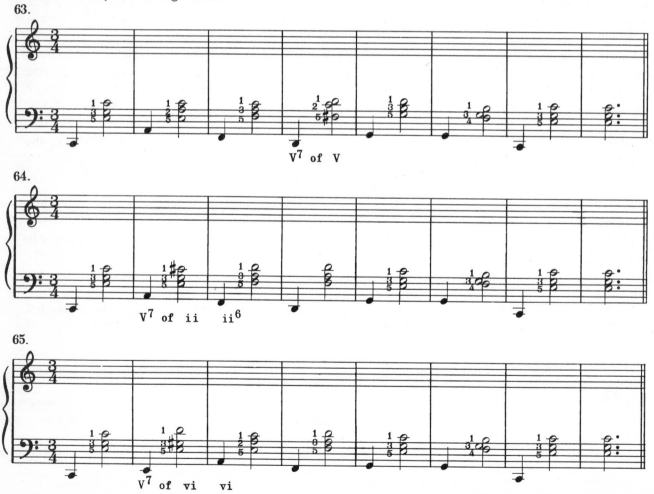

PART III

Melodies to Be Harmonized and Transposed

In this part there are over *forty melodies* that can be *easily harmonized* with one, two, three, or more chords. They are divided into groups: those that can be harmonized with one or two chords, those that can be harmonized with three chords, and those that should be harmonized with four or more chords.

Examples of simple accompaniments with melodies are on page **56**. Rhythmic variations suitable for accompaniments are on pages 52, 53, 54, 55. Other chord progressions arranged for this kind of harmonization are included in the keyboard harmony part and are on pages 41, 43, 44, 45, 47, 48, 50. Chords to be used are marked by their Roman numeral names and are found under the melody note as they occur in the melody. Only changes in chords are marked. The rhythmic variations of the chords and chord positions to be played are to be worked out by the student.

When planning the accompaniments for a melody several things should be considered. The *spirit* of the melody should be matched with an appropriate accompaniment. The *tempo* of the melody influences the kind of rhythmic pattern to be used. A *fast melody* will ordinarily have few changes in chords and a rather slow-moving accompaniment. A *slow melody* will need more movement and variation in the accompaniment.

Rhythmic patterns vary. *Block chords* are the easiest for the beginner to use. Played regularly on the accented beats they make a strong, rhythmic, harmonic accompaniment.

Broken chords can be varied in note combinations and in rhythm.

The accompaniment generally harmonizes with the *melody tones* on the strong beats (one in 3/4 meter, one and three in 4/4 meter, one and four in 6/8 meter). A melody note on a strong beat should ordinarily be found in the chord. Occasionally a non-chord tone (marked +) is found on a strong beat but will generally resolve immediately to a chord tone.

Melodies are to be *harmonized* in the original key, then *transposed* to other keys. Generally melodies are transposed to suit the voice of the singer. A half step or one full step up or down is quite often sufficient to put a melody in a comfortable singing range. However, some songs may need to be transposed up or down a third, fourth, or fifth. The highest and lowest notes indicate the *range* of the melody and should serve as a guide for choosing the appropriate key.

When preparing to transpose a melody, establish the new key by reviewing the scale pattern, signature, and chord progressions. Then, find the new melody note on which to begin. The melody and chords in the new key will have the same relationship to each other that they had to each other in the original key. The only difference will be that they will now sound either higher or lower than before.

Planning interesting and varied harmonizations for easy melodies builds a sense of discrimination and **taste** in arranging accompaniment patterns. It is important to harmonize many easy melodies before attempting more difficult ones. The easiest melodies generally fall in a five or six note position under the hand and can be harmonized with two or three chords. More difficult melodies move from one hand position to another. In this case the chord patterns may have to be shifted to another position (inversion) to keep melody and accompaniment from overlapping. When a melody note is duplicated in the chord, the the melody note should be given the preference and played as such.

Accompaniment Pattern

Rhythmic Variations suitable for use in harmonizing melodies.

These can be adapted for any chord progression.

THREE VOICE, BASS CLEF CHORD PROGRESSIONS suitable for accompanying melodies in Part III can be found on the following pages:

(1) I IV I — three positions, page 39

(2) I V I — three positions, page 40

(3) I IV V I — three positions, page 41

(4) I V7 I — three positions, page 43

(5) I IV V7 I — three positions, page 44

(6) Chord progressions with a waltz bass — I IV V7 I — three positions, page 44

(7) I IV ii V7 I — one position, page 45

(8) Secondary dominants — V of IV, V of V, V of ii, V of Vi, V of iii, page 48

When a melody is familiar and the singer does not need the melody to be played, the piano arrangement may consist entirely of chord patterns (progressions). Examples of these, to be played, transposed, and used with familiar melodies given are below:

Waltz Bass in Three Positions

Soprano Melody

Bass Melody

Alto Melody (thumb melody)

An Example of a Simple Song and Accompaniment.

Summm, Summ, Summ

German Folk Song

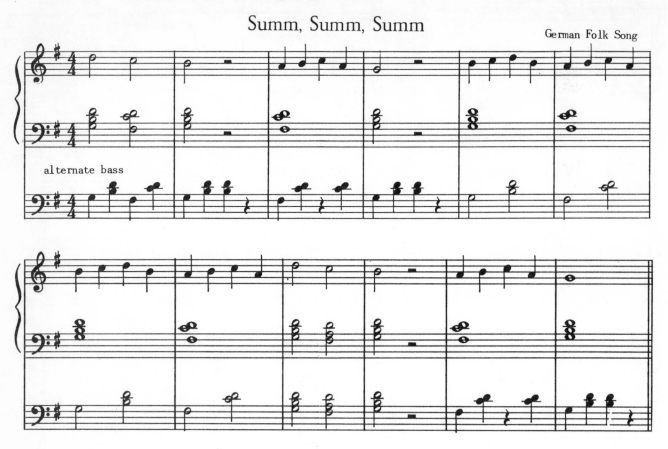

alternate bass

Summ, Summ, Summ

Transposed to the Key of F.

Melodies to Be Harmonized
With Two Chords

The melodies in this group can be harmonized with one or two of the following chords:

I, i, IV, iv, V, V7

Although the inversions are not indicated, the following chord positions are appropriate:

I, i, IV_4^6, iv_4^6, V_3^6, V_5^6

(+ indicates a non-chord tone)

Bugle Call (Mess Call)

Bugle Call (Taps)

Frère Jacques

French Folk Song

Thankfulness

Old English Round

River, Little River

Old Tune

River, River Little River

(Minor mode)

Row, Row, Row Your Boat

Round

When accompanying singing, fast melody notes may be left out and a long, accented note substituted.

An Old Tune (I Had a Cat)

London Bridge

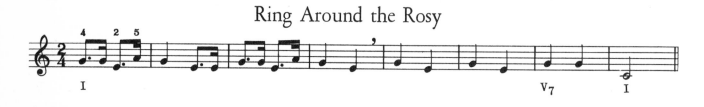

Ring Around the Rosy

Skip to My Lou

58

Go Tell Aunt Rhody

Cuckoo (German Folk Tune)

Lightly Row

English Folk Tune

The Laughing Song

O Where, O Where Has My Little Dog Gone?

German Folk Song

Patapan

Burgundian Carol

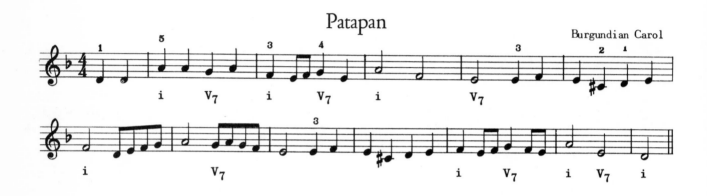

O How Lovely Is the Evening (Round)

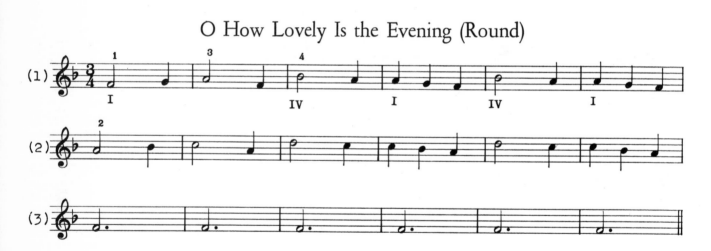

Melodies to Be Harmonized
With Three Chords

The melodies in this group can be harmonized with three of the following chords:

I, i, IV, iv, V, V7

Although the inversions are not indicated, the following chord positions are appropriate:

I, i, IV_4^6, iv_4^6, V_3^6, V_5^6

(+ indicates a non-chord tone)

Hickory Dickory Dock

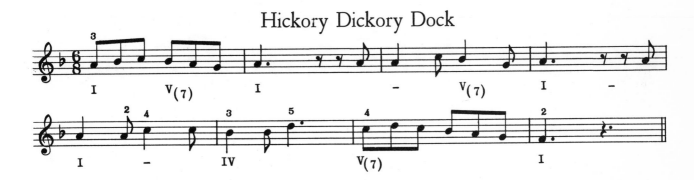

Baa Baa Black Sheep

Twinkle Twinkle Little Star

She'll Be Comin' Round the Mountain When She Comes

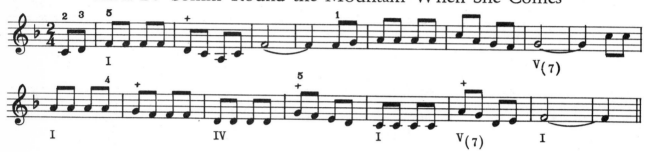

O Susanna

Stephen Foster

For He's A Jolly Good Fellow

63

Silent Night

F. Grüber

Dona Nobis Pacem (canon)

On Top of Old Smoky

Kentucky Folk Song

64

The Old Brass Wagon

American Folk Song

The Arkansas Traveler

American

65

Melodies to Be Harmonized With Four or More Chords

For the harmonization of the melodies in this group, a variety of diatonic triads and dominant sevenths, including secondary dominants, are used. Some of these melodies, completely harmonized in three part harmony, are also included in Part VI, *Songs to Play and Sing*. Only the chord function is indicated; inversions and seventh chords may be elected. The pianistic idiom, which permits more or less than four parts, may be used.

We Gather Together

Netherlands Tune

Lullaby

J. Brahms

Dixie

Dan Emmett

Home on the Range

Cowboy Song

Au Clair de la Lune

French Folk Tune

English Folk Tune

Jingle Bells

The Ash Grove

Welsh Folk Tune

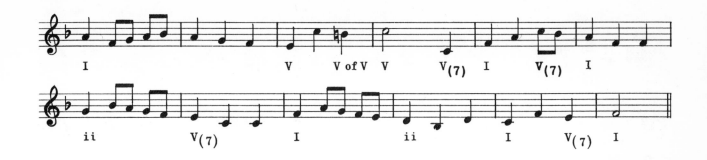

When Johnny Comes Marching Home

Louis Lambert

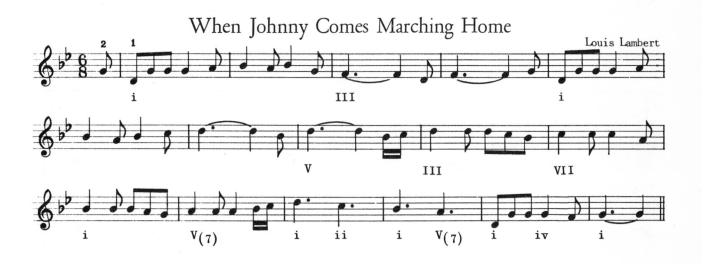

Jeanie With the Light Brown Hair

S. Foster

**PART IV**

Basic Exercises for the Development of Coordination and Technique

Development of legato playing
Independence of fingers
Keeping an even tempo
Moving the thumb under
Accuracy of attack
Changing fingers while holding down notes
Developing speed and facility
Playing two or more independent melodies contrapuntally
Playing repeated notes accurately and evenly
Accuracy in playing sequences of triads and sevenths chords

Additional exercises on scales and chords can be found in the sections on scales and keyboard harmony.

Each exercise is accompanied by suggestions for its use. However, for an extended study of these exercises refer to the *Study Guide,* page 150.

EXERCISE   1   For Legato Playing

Sustain each note until the instant the next note is played.

For Staccato playing
Release each note quickly.

Repeat three times (in half notes, quarter notes, and in eighth notes).

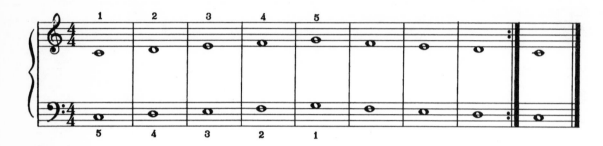

EXERCISE   2   For Independence of Fingers

Play slowly.   Repeat several times increasing the speed each time.

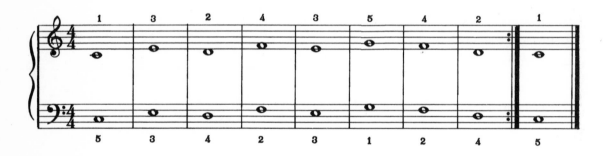

EXERCISE   3   For Practice in Playing Consecutive Thirds

Play slowly.   Repeat several times increasing the speed each time.

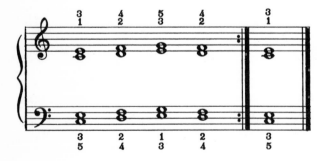

72

EXERCISE 4 For Playing Rhythmic Patterns Containing Different Note Values
Play each note firmly.

Practice with metronome at the following speeds:

♩ = 60   ♩ = 120   ♩ = 160

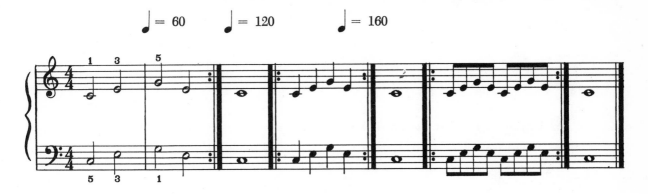

EXERCISE 5 For Moving Thumb Under Smoothly
Keep a relaxed arm while playing.

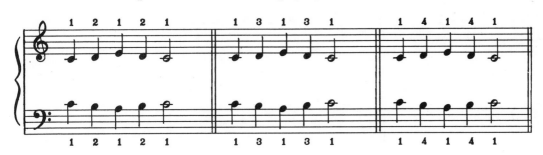

EXERCISE 6 For Moving Thumb Under Smoothly
Let the thumb do the work.

EXERCISE   7 For Accuracy of Attack With Any Finger

Practice using other fingers.
Right hand: (2)   (3)   (4)   (5)
Left hand: (4)   (3)   (2)   (1)

EXERCISE   8 For Playing Skips and Step-wise Progressions with Accuracy and Clarity
            Play in other keys.

EXERCISE   9 For Improving Accuracy in Attack
            Repeat four times changing fingers each time.
            Practice on other white notes.
            Practice on black notes.
            Vary the rhythm.

74

EXERCISE 10 For Improving Accuracy in Attack

Play the entire exercise with the right hand. (Fingers 1 3 5)
Play the entire exercise with the left hand. (Fingers 5 3 1)
Play the entire exercise with alternating hands.
Repeat on all major and minor triads.

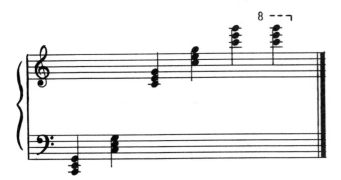

EXERCISE 11 For Changing Fingers While Holding Down the Note

Hold the note all the way down so that it continues to sound.

EXERCISE 12 For Changing Fingers While Holding Down Notes

Start with the fingers indicated. Change fingers while holding down the notes and proceed, playing each note with the fingering used on the first note. Keep strict time while playing.

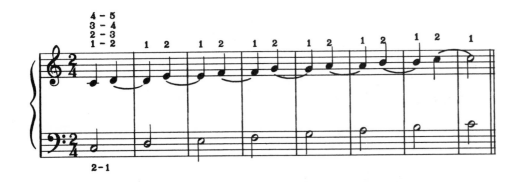

EXERCISE 13 For Holding Down Some Fingers While Playing a Rhythmic Pattern with Others
Keep rhythm steady.
Do not release notes until tie is over.
Hold notes down firmly.

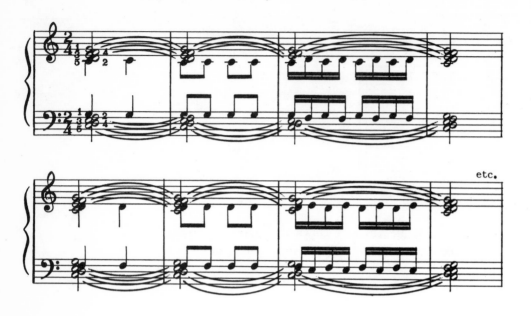

EXERCISE 14 For Developing Independence of Voices
Practice with metronome. ♩ = 60 and ♩ = 120.

EXERCISE 15 For Developing Independence of Voices (Contrapuntal Style)
Play with high fingers.
Practice at different speeds.
Play in other keys.

76

EXERCISE 16 For Playing with Speed and Facility

♩ = 184 m.m.

EXERCISE 17 For Playing Scale Intervals with Ease

The first note after each bar is a scale tone.
Continue the pattern up the entire scale of C Major.
TRANSPOSE

The first note after each bar is a scale tone.
Continue the pattern up the entire scale of C Major.
TRANSPOSE

EXERCISE 18 For Playing Repeated Notes Evenly

EXERCISE 19 For Facility and Clarity in Playing Single Notes

Start each two measure pattern on a scale tone continuing to the top of the scale.
Transpose to other keys both major and minor.

EXERCISE 20 A Variation of Exercise 19

78

Major and Minor Triads

(ascending and descending chromatically)

A Study in Reading, Playing, and Hearing These Chords.

Suggested Fingerings:

(a) R. H.
```
        5   4
        3 or 2   (up and back)          L. H.   3 or 2
        1   1                                   5   4
```
```
                                                1   1
```

(b) for legato (sliding the thumb)

```
        4 3 4 3 4 5 3 4 3 4 5 3                 1 1 1 2 1 1 2 1 2 1 1 2 1
  R. H. 2 2 2 2 2 2 2 2 2 2 2 2          L. H.  2 2 2 3 2 2 3 2 3 2 2 3 2
        1 1 1 1 1 1 1 1 1 1 1 1                 4 3 4 5 5 4 5 4 5 4 5 4 3 5 4
```

79

Seventh Chords

(ascending and descending chromatically)

A Study in Reading, Playing, and Hearing These Chords.

Suggested Fingerings:

		4	5			1
(a)	R. H.	3	or 3		L. H.	2
		2	2			3
		1	1			5

					1
(b)	For Legato				2
	R. H. (top voice) 4 5 4 5 etc.		L. H.	3
					5

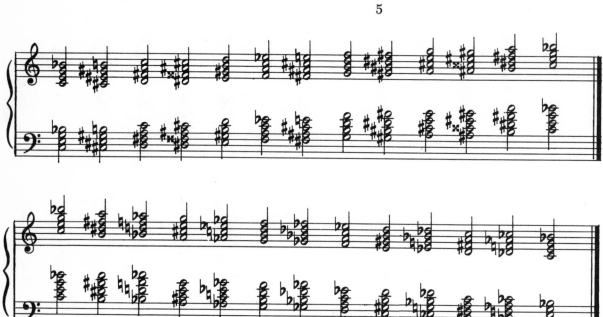

PART V

The Pedals[1]

[1]Damper Pedal (Ped.), Sostenuto Pedal (Sost.), (Tone Sustaining Pedal — T. S. A.), Una Corda Pedal (u. c.).

(The Right Pedal)
Damper Pedal

(Use right foot, heel on the floor.)

This is called the damper pedal because when it is pressed down the dampers are released (held back) from the strings and the sound is sustained.

Its chief function is to produce a legato effect. However, it is sometimes used for emphasis.

Legato Pedal Exercise

Release the pedal as the note is played and immediately press down again. This produces a good legato.

Accent Pedal (tap) Exercise

Press down the pedal as the note is played and release it when the note is released. This emphasizes the note and helps establish a strong rhythmic pattern.

Improvisation Using the Damper Pedal

1. On the Pentatonic Scale

Interesting blends of tones can be produced by developing melodies on the pentatonic scale (black notes, see page 21), while holding down the damper pedal.

2. On the Whole Tone Scale

With the whole tone scale as a subject, improvise a sequence of whole tone patterns holding down the damper pedal throughout. Vary this by using high and low registers and by changing the rhythm.

(The Middle Pedal)
Sostenuto Pedal*

When the sostenuto pedal on a grand piano is depressed it raises the dampers from the notes that are *already being held* but allows the dampers to drop naturally, without being sustained, on any notes *sounded after* the pedal is depressed.

*Called the *Tone Sustaining Pedal* by Bela Bartok in his *Mikrokosmos*.

On most upright pianos the sostenuto pedal works like the damper pedal but extends only over the lower register.

Sostenuto Pedal Example

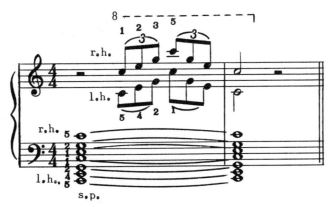

Use right foot.

Improvisation Using the Sostenuto Pedal

By holding down one chord with the sostenuto pedal and improvising on another chord or scale at the same time, a study in "polytonality" can be developed. Some combinations to use are:

Hold in low register	Improvise on in a high register
C chord	G7 chord
C chord	F (of f minor) chord
G7 chord	D7 chord
c chord	c minor scale (melodic form)

(The Left Pedal)
Una Corda Pedal

When the una corda (one string) pedal is depressed on a grand piano the keyboard action and hammers are shifted to the right* so that the hammers strike two of the three identically tuned strings in the middle and upper registers and one of the two identically tuned strings in the lowest register. This is only a slight modification of the original una corda principal. While it reduces the volume, it is really meant to give a change of timbre. On an upright piano the same effect is produced by different means, generally by reducing the leverage between the hammers and the strings. (It lifts the hammer rail to shorten the hammer stroke.)

The term tre corde (t. c.) means to release the *una cords* (u. c.) pedal.

Una Corda Pedal Example

from "All Through the Night"

*On all but very, very old pianos. On a few grand pianos the pedal operates like an upright.

PART VI

Piano Adaptations of Instrumental and Vocal Music

Appreciation of Music of Various Media by Use of the Piano

By playing themes and harmonies from instrumental and vocal literature, the pianist is using the keyboard as a tool for understanding and enjoying these other kinds of music.

Examples of seven kinds of music have been arranged so that they can be played on the keyboard. Included are:

Three Chorales
Three Operas
Two Oratorios
Five Symphonies
One Symphonic Poem
One Theme and Variation
One Suite

The study of this part will be made more meaningful with the following enrichments:

1. Listening to the recordings of the music in its original form (or attendance at performances of the music).
2. Following the musical scores of the composition.
3. Gathering historical, biographical, and musical information about the music and the composers.

Three different study approaches are recommended for the study of this section:

1. Chronological Study by Composers: Bach, Handel, Haydn, Mozart, Beethoven, Schubert, Wagner, Franck, Brahms, Bizet, Humperdinck, Strauss.
2. A Study by Musical Areas: Chorales, Operas, Oratorios, Symphonies, the Symphonic Poem, a Theme and Variations, a Suite.
3. A Progressive Study of Compositions According to Technical Difficulties on the Keyboard (as arranged here):

   Symphony No. 9 in D Minor Op. 125 — Beethoven
   The Creation — Haydn

My Heart Ever Faithful — Bach
Don Giovanni — Mozart
Symphony in D Minor — Franck
Symphony No. 8 — Schubert
Variations on a Theme by Haydn — Brahms
Hansel and Gretel — Humperdinck
The Messiah — Handel
Chorale No. 42 — Bach
Symphony No. 1 — Haydn
Symphony No. 40 — Mozart
Chorale No. 54 — Bach
Till Eulenspiegel Op. 28 — R. Strauss
Die Meistersinger — Wagner
L'Arlésienne Suite No. 1 and 2 — Bizet

Adaptations for Piano*

Bach

My Heart Ever Faithful (Cantata No. 68)
Chorale No. 42
Chorale No. 54

Handel

The Messiah

Haydn

Symphony No. 101 in D Major
The Creation

Mozart

Symphony No. 40 in g minor K. 550
Don Giovanni

Beethoven

Symphony No. 9

Schubert

Symphony in b minor No. 8

Wagner

Die Meistersinger

Franck

Symphony No. 1 in d minor

Brahms

Variation on a Theme by Haydn

Bizet

L'Arlésienne Suite No. 1 and No. 2

Humperdinck

Hänsel and Gretel

Strauss, R.

Till Eulenspiegel Op. 28

*Composers listed chronologically.

86

My Heart Ever Faithful

from

Cantata No. 68
Also hat Gott die Welt geliebt

J. S. Bach

Chorale No. 42

Du Friedensfürst, Herr, Jesu Christ
J. S. Bach

(Full Realization)

Chorale No. 54

Lobt Gott, ihr Christen, allzugleich.
J. S. Bach

(Partial Realization)

He Shall Feed His Flock Like a Shepherd

Air for Alto

from

"The Messiah" (part 1)

George Frederich Handel

How Beautiful Are the Feet of Them

Air for Soprano

from

"The Messiah" (part 2)

George Frederich Handel

A chorale with partial realization

89

I Know That My Redeemer Liveth

Air for Soprano

from

"The Messiah" (part 3)

George Frederich Handel

Symphony No. 101 in D Major, "The Clock" (1794)

Franz Josef Haydn

from First Movement

from Third Movement

Menuetto

Symphony No. 101 in D Major, "The Clock" (1794)

Franz Josef Haydn

from Fourth Movement

Vivace

With Verdure Clad (solo for soprano)
from "The Creation"

Franz Joseph Haydn

The Heavens Are Telling (trio and chorus)
from "The Creation"

Franz Josef Haydn

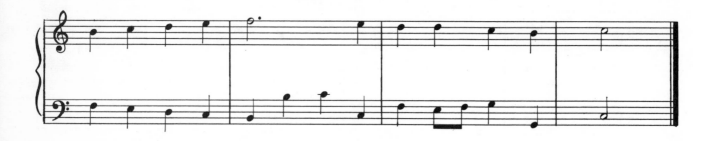

On Thee Each Living Soul Awaits (duet for soprano and tenor)
from "The Creation"

Franz Josef Haydn

1. Play left hand one octave lower
   or
2. Play as a duet on two pianos
   or
3. Play one part while the other part is sung.

Symphony No. 40 in G Minor (K550) (1788)

Wolfgang Amadeus Mozart

from First Movement (second theme)

Symphony No. 40 in G Minor (K550) (1788)

Wolfgang Amadeus Mozart

from Third Movement

Symphony No. 40 in G Minor (K550) (1788)

Wolfgang Amadeus Mozart

from Fourth Movement

Don Giovanni

an opera in two acts

by

Wolfgang Amadeus Mozart
(first performance 1787)

Notte e giorno faticar (Leporello)
from Act 1

96

Don Giovanni (continued)

Wolfgang Amadeus Mozart

La ci darem la mano (Don Giovanni, Zerlina)
from Act 1

97

Don Giovanni (continued)

Wolfgang Amadeus Mozart

Batti, batti, o bel Masetto (Zerlina) (aria)
from Act 1

Il miotesoro intanto (Don Octavio) (aria)
from Act 2

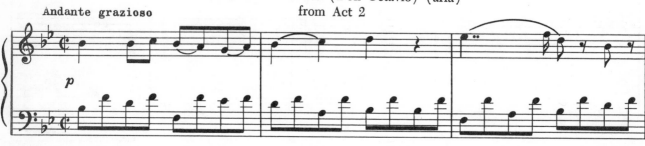

Symphony No. 9 in D Minor Op. 125 (1824)

Ludwig van Beethoven

from First Movement (first theme)

98

Symphony No. 9 in D Minor Op. 125 (continued)

Ludwig van Beethoven

from Second Movement
Trio all breve

Symphony No. 9 in D Minor Op. 125 (continued)

Ludwig van Beethoven

from Fourth Movement (Theme and Variations)
with Chorale Finale on Schiller's *"Ode to Joy"*

(Baritone Recitative)

O BROTHERS, THESE SAD TONES NO LONGER!
RATHER RAISE WE NOW TOGETHER OUR VOICES,
AND JOYFUL BE OUR SONG!

First theme — (to be harmonized by student)

Second theme

Andante maestoso

basses and tenors

Symphony No. 8 in B Minor "Unfinished" (1822)

Franz Peter Schubert

from First Movement

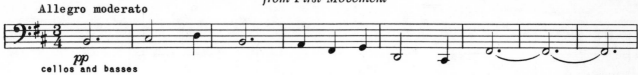

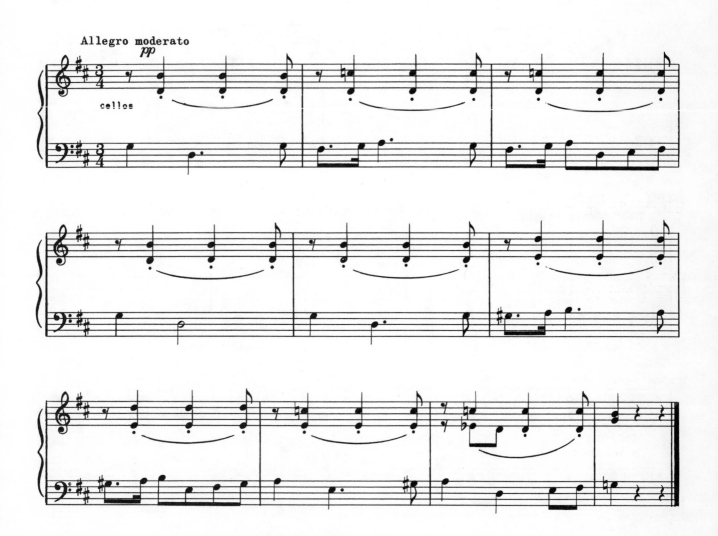

Die Meistersinger von Nürnberg (Munich, 1868)

Richard Wagner

Prelude to Act III

Prelude to Act I

Die Meistersinger von Nürnberg (continued)

Prelude to Act I

for next phrase transpose first five measures to G Major.

Prelude to Act I

Variations on a Theme by Joseph Haydn

Johannes Brahms, Opus 56a

Chorale St. Antoni

Andante

Variation No. 3

Symphony in D Minor (1886-1888)

César Franck

FIRST MOVEMENT

Theme I

Theme II

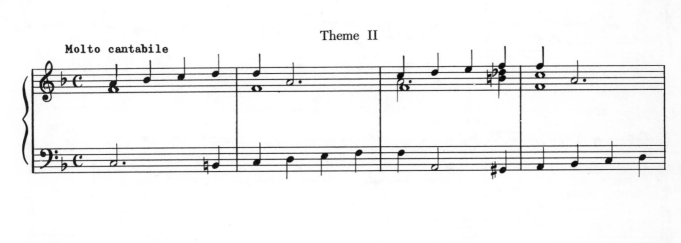

Symphony in D Minor (continued)

FIRST MOVEMENT

Theme III

Theme III

Symphony in D Minor (continued)

SECOND MOVEMENT

Theme I

SECOND MOVEMENT

Theme III

L` Arlesienne Suite No. 1

Georges Bizet

I PRELUDE

(to be harmonized by the student)

IV CARILLON

L' Arlesienne Suite No. 2

Georges Bizet

I PASTORALE

Andante moderato

II INTERMEZZO

Andante moderato

L' Arlesienne Suite No. 2 (continued)

Georges Bizet

III MINUETTO

Andantino

IV FARANDOLE

Allegro vivo e deciso

Hänsel and Gretel (an opera in three acts) 1895

E. Humperdinck

FOLK SONG

Act. I (Gretel)

Act I LITTLE BROTHER, DANCE WITH ME (Gretel)

110

PRELUDE TO ACT II WITCHES RIDE

Hänsel and Gretel (continued)

THE CUCKOO

Act II Scene I

(Cuckoo instrument answered by Hänsel, then Gretel)

LITTLE MAN IN THE WOOD

Act II Scene I (Gretel)

Hänsel and Gretel (continued)

FOURTEEN ANGELS WATCH DO KEEP

Act II   Scene II

Hänsel and Gretel (continued)

THE SANDMAN

Act II   Scene II

Moderato

HOCUS POCUS

Act III   Scene III

Piu tranquillo

THE WITCH VALSE

Act III   Scene IV

"Till Eulenspiegels lustige Streiche" Opus 28
"The Merry Pranks of Till Eulenspiegel"

1895

A symphonic poem in free rondo style

by

Richard Strauss

Till's Themes

PART VII

Songs to Play and Sing*

The songs in this section have been chosen for their widely diversified character and for their importance to this phase of American music. Included are three patriotic songs, one song of thanksgiving, a hymn tune, a Negro spiritual, an American cowboy song, an American marching song, and three songs emphasizing the Anglo-Saxon background of American music.

*In easy and moderately easy three part settings, arranged by Alexander Post.

Suggestions for Playing These Songs

Although playing for group singing is the primary concern here, the suggestions apply equally well to playing for vocal or instrumental solos or small ensembles.

When playing for group singing, the melody should be brought out above the accompanying harmonies. The melody should stand out as if being sung. A deep legato touch will help to produce this effect. Phrasing should at all times coincide with the words of the song. Not only must the pianist follow the music but he also must follow the words. The dynamics of the playing should be controlled by the singers.

The last phrase of the song may be played for an introduction. This establishes the key and sets the tempo and style of the song.

Analysis of these accompaniments can be developed into a profitable study by correlating it with Part Two, *Formal Keyboard Exercises*. For improvising other accompaniments, suggestions can be found in Part Three, *Informal Harmonization and Transposition of Melodies*. The following songs will be found in Part Three, with chord symbols: *The Ash Grove, Home on the Range, We Gather Together,* and *When Johnny Comes Marching Home.*

America

My country, 'tis of thee,
Sweet land of liberty, Of thee I sing.
Land where my fathers died! Land of the pilgrim's pride!
From ev'ry mountainside, Let freedom ring!

My native country, thee,
Land of the noble free, Thy name I love.
I love thy rocks and rills, Thy woods and templed hills;
My heart with rapture thrills Like that above.

Let music swell the breeze,
And ring from all the trees Sweet freedom's song.
Let mortal tongues awake; Let all that breathe partake;
Let rocks their silence break, — The sound prolong.

Our fathers' God, to Thee,
Author of liberty, To Thee we sing.
Long may our land be bright With freedom's holy light;
Protect us by Thy might, Great God, our King!

England and the United States are at least two countries which make use of this tune for their national hymn. England's "God Save the King" has different words but the same melody. Some sources give Henry Carey (1690-1743), an Englishman, credit for having written the tune, though parts of it have been traced back to Dr. John Bull (1563-1628). The words were written in 1832 by Reverend S. F. Smith, an American clergyman. The song was first sung publicly that same year at a children's celebration, July 4, in Boston.

America

Samuel F. Smith

Henry Carey

*Transpose to the key of F for lower voices.

America, The Beautiful

O beautiful for spacious skies, For amber waves of grain,
For purple mountain majesties Above the fruited plain.
America! America! God shed His grace on thee,
And crown thy good with brotherhood From sea to shining sea.

O beautiful for pilgrim feet Whose stern impassioned stress
A thoroughfare for freedom beat Across the wilderness.
America! America! God mend thine ev'ry flaw,
Confirm thy soul in self-control, Thy liberty in law.

O beautiful for heroes proved In liberating strife,
Who more than self their country loved, And mercy more than life.
America! America! May God thy gold refine
Till all success be nobleness And ev'ry gain divine.

O beautiful for patriot dream That sees beyond the years
Thine alabaster cities gleam Undimmed by human tears.
America! America! God shed His grace on thee,
And crown thy good with brotherhood From sea to shining sea.

This is one of our most worthy patriotic songs. The music was written by an American, Samuel A. Ward, who died in 1903. The words were composed by a professor of English in Wellesley College, Katherine Lee Bates.

America, The Beautiful

Katherine Lee Bates

Samuel A. Ward

*Transpose to the key of B Flat.

The Star-Spangled Banner

O say! can you see, by the dawn's early light,
What so proudly we hail'd at the twilight's last gleaming?
Whose broad stripes and bright stars, thro' the perilous fight,
O'er the ramparts we watch'd, were so gallantly streaming?
And the rockets' red glare, the bombs bursting in air,
Gave proof thro' the night that our flag was still there.
O say, does that Star-spangled Banner yet wave
O'er the land of the free and the home of the brave?

O thus be it ever when freemen shall stand
Between their loved homes and the war's desolation!
Blest with vict'ry and peace, may the heav'n-rescued land
Praise the Pow'r that hath made and preserved us a nation!
Then conquer we must, when our cause it is just,
And this be our motto: "In God is our trust!"
And the Star-spangled Banner in triumph shall wave
O'er the land of the free and the home of the brave!

The words to this song were written by Francis Scott Key in 1814 during the War of 1812 between England and the United States. The author was held on a British ship while it bombarded Fort McHenry. He noticed when morning came that "our flag was still there," and was inspired to write these stirring words. This has become our national anthem.

The Star-Spangled Banner

John Stafford Smith

Francis Scott Key

*Transpose to the Key of A Flat.

We Gather Together

We gather together to ask the Lord's blessing,
He chastens and hastens His will to make known;
The wicked oppressing now cease from distressing,
Sing praises to His name, He forgets not His own.

Beside us to guide us, our God with us joining,
Ordaining, maintaining His kingdom divine,
So from the beginning the fight we were winning;
Thou, Lord, wast at our side, all glory be Thine.

We all do extol Thee, Thou leader triumphant,
And pray that Thou still our defender will be,
Let Thy congregation escape tribulation,
Thy name be ever praised O Lord, make us free.

This majestic song, dating back three hundred years, is said to have been sung by the Dutch people as a Hymn of Thanksgiving for their liberation from Spanish oppression. It is popularly known as a Thanksgiving song throughout the United States, in commemoration of the Pilgrims' first harvest. The piano accompaniment to this song should be played in the solid, dignified style of a hymn.

We Gather Together

Traditional Netherlands Tune

Greensleeves

The old year now away is fled, The new year it is entered,
Then let us now our sins down tread and joyfully all appear.

Refrain:
Let's merry be this day And let us now both sport and play.
Hang grief, cast away, God send you happy new year.

And now, with New Year's, gifts each friend Unto each other they do send.
God grant we may all our lives amend, and that the truth may appear.

This smoothly swinging pastorale tune is a "Wait's Carol" dating back to the Middle Ages. Waits were night guards, stationed at the city gates of London, who occasionally sang and danced for the nobility at Christmas time. Originally, this carol was a round dance in which the dancers sang the tune themselves. Sometimes they were accompanied by recorders, a small drum and a lute. A piano accompaniment could be improvised, imitating a lute accompaniment in Dorian mode.

"Greensleeves" is mentioned by Shakespeare in "The Merry Wives of Windsor" and it is also used in "The Beggar's Opera" by John Gay (1727). Vaughn-Williams has used "Greensleeves" in his opera, "Sir John in Love," and in his "Greensleeves Fantasy."

Greensleeves

English Folk Song

When Johnny Comes Marching Home

When Johnny comes marching home again, Hurrah! Hurrah!
We'll give him a hearty welcome then, Hurrah! Hurrah!
The men will cheer, the boys will shout, The ladies they will all turn out.
And we'll all feel gay when Johnny comes marching home.

The old church bell will peal with joy, Hurrah! Hurrah!
To welcome home our darling boy, Hurrah! Hurrah!
The village lads and lassies gay With roses they will strew the way
And we'll all feel gay When Johnny comes marching home.

Get ready for the jubilee, Hurrah! Hurrah!
We'll give the heroes three times three, Hurrah! Hurrah!
The laurel wreath is ready now To place upon his loyal brow,
And we'll all feel gay When Johnny comes marching home!

Although this song dates back to the Civil War, it did not become well known until it was popularized by American Bandmaster Patrick Gilmore, at the outbreak of the Spanish American War in 1898. The vigorous marching swing of this melody lends itself to the typical 6/8 accompaniment with a drum-like accent at the beginning of each measure. Notice the abrupt changes from G minor to B flat major. "When Johnny Comes Marching Home" appears in theme and variations form in "The American Salute" by Morton Gould.

126

When Johnny Comes Marching Home

Louis Lambert

127

Drink to Me With Only Thine Eyes

Drink to me only with thine eyes, And I will pledge with mine,
Or leave a kiss within the cup, And I'll not ask for wine;
The thirst that from the soul doth rise Doth ask a drink divine;
But might I of Jove's nectar sup I would not change for thine.

I sent thee late a rosy wreath, Not so much hon'ring thee,
As giving it a hope that there It could not withered be;
But thou there-on didst only breathe And send'st it back to me;
Since when it grows and smells I swear, Not of itself but thee.

The words for this song come from a poem, "To Celia," written by a great
English dramatist, Ben Jonson (1573-1637), who lived at the time of Shakespeare.

Drink to Me With Only Thine Eyes

Old English Air

The Ash Grove

The ash grove, how graceful, how plainly 'tis speaking,
The harp through its playing has language for me.
When over its branches the sunlight is breaking,
A host of kind faces is gazing on me.
The friends of my childhood again are before me,
Each step wakes a mem'ry, as freely I roam.
With soft whispers laden, its leaves rustle o'er me;
The ash grove, the ash grove alone is my home.

My laughter is over, my step loses lightness,
Old country-side measures steal soft on my ear;
I only remember the past and its brightness;
The dear ones I mourn for again gather here.
From ev'ry dark nook they press forward to meet me,
I lift up my eyes to the broad leafy dome;
And others are there, looking downward to greet me;
The ash grove, the ash grove alone is my home.

This smoothly flowing melody is of Welsh origin and was originally entitled "Llyn On." Since Welsh music was frequently accompanied by the harp, it would be appropriate to improvise a harp-like accompaniment. The beautiful grace of this melody lends itself to the Welsh Eisteddfods (singing festivals) which date back to the twelfth century.

The Ash Grove

Old Welsh Air

Home on the Range

O give me a home where the buffaloes roam,
Where the deer and the antelope play,
Where seldom is heard a discouraging word,
And the skies are not cloudy all day.

Refrain:
Home, home on the range,
Where the deer and the antelope play,
Where seldom is heard A discouraging word,
And the skies are not cloudy all day.

How often at night when the heavens are bright,
With the light from the glittering stars,
Have I stood there amazed and asked, as I gazed,
If their glory exceeds that of ours.

The easy 3-4 swing of this melody depicts the moods of the lone cowboy, riding along the Western Plain. Although it was published as early as 1910, it did not become well known until it was popularized by the radio in the 1930's, when a half-million dollar copyright suit was brought for the publication of this song. This melody can be accompanied at the piano with an improvised guitar-like strumming effect. Morton Gould has used this melody in his "Cowboy Rhapsody."

132

Home on the Range

Swing Low, Sweet Chariot

Swing low, sweet chariot, Comin' for to carry me home!
Swing low, sweet chariot, Comin' for to carry me home!
I looked over Jordan an' what did I see, Comin' for to carry me home!
A band of angels comin' after me, Comin' for to carry me home!

Swing low, sweet chariot, Comin' for to carry me home!
Swing low, sweet chariot, Comin' for to carry me home!
If you get there before I do, Comin' for to carry me home!
Jess tell my frien's that I'm acomin' too, Comin' for to carry me home!

Swing low, sweet chariot, Comin' for to carry me home!
Swing low, sweet chariot, Comin' for to carry me home!
I'm sometimes up an' sometimes down, Comin' for to carry me home!
But still my soul feels heavenly boun', Comin' for to carry me home!

This is one of the best-known Negro spirituals. Inherent in the words are the fervor and emotion characteristic of all spirituals. The single melodic line was originally sung by a soloist and the harmony part by a chorus.

Swing Low, Sweet Chariot

O Come, All Ye Faithful

Adeste Fideles

O come, all ye faithful, joyful and triumphant,
O come ye, O come ye to Bethlehem:
Come and behold Him, born the king of angels:
O come, let us adore Him, O come, let us adore Him,
O come, let us adore Him, Christ the Lord.

Adeste fideles, laeti triumphantes,
Venite, Venite, in Bethlehem:
Natum videte, Regem angelorum:
Venite adoremus, Venite adoremus,
Venite adoremus, Dominum.

The origin of this tune is not known. The words are attributed to various sources: Reading, Thurley, and to the Cistercian monks. The words come from an old Latin hymn of the eighteenth century, "Adeste Fideles."

O Come, All Ye Faithful

PART VIII

Listening Guide for Standard Piano Compositions

This list of piano compositions is to help you increase your appreciation of piano literature. Most of it is played frequently on recital programs and is obtainable on recordings. These are selections which piano students should learn to recognize when they hear them. Following the scores while listening to the recordings is very helpful. Listening to much piano music of this type builds respect for, and an understanding of, the piano as a concert instrument.

For more interesting and varied listening, the selections have been arranged in program groups representing different centuries, styles, and composers. Pertinent information, such as dates and biographical data, national traits, the form of composition, style characteristics of certain composers, etc., should be found in musical encyclopedias.

The study of this chapter can be organized in various ways: one program at a time; one composer at a time; one period at a time. In any case, when possible, scores should be followed and background material should be reviewed.

Standard Piano Compositions for Listening*

Sonata in A Minor 429 — D. Scarlatti
Rondo in D Major — K485 — W. A. Mozart
Sonata in B Flat Major (posthumous) — F. Schubert
Ritual Fire Dance — M. de Falla
Le Petit Ane Blanc — J. Ibert

Prelude and Fugue in B Flat Minor, vol. 1, Well Tempered Clavier—J. S. Bach
Sonata in C Major Op. 53 (Waldstein) — L. Beethoven
Prelude in G Minor — Rachmaninoff
Children's Corner Suite — C. Debussy

Partita No. 2 in C Minor — J. S. Bach
Sonata in A Major Op. 120 — F. Schubert
Intermezzo in B Flat Minor Op. 117, No. 2 — J. Brahms
Etude in C Minor Op. 10, No. 12 (Revolutionary) — F. Chopin
Concerto in A Minor — R. Schumann

Prelude and Fugue in C Major, vol. 1, W.T.C. — J. S. Bach
Sonata in F Minor Op. 57 (Appassionata) — L. Beethoven
Prelude in C Major Op. 28, No. 1 — F. Chopin
Fantasy Impromptu Op. 66 — F. Chopin
Six Little Piano Pieces — A. Schoenberg
Feux d'artifice — Debussy

Sonata in D Major — Haydn
Rondo Capriccioso Op. 14 — Mendelssohn
Etude in G Flat Minor Op. 10, No. 5 (Black Key) — Chopin
Waltz in A Flat Op. 42 — Chopin
Woodland Sketches — MacDowell
Cat and Mouse — Debussy

Prelude and Fugue in B Flat Major vol. 1, W.T.C. — J. S. Bach
Carnaval Op. 9 — Schumann
Nocturne in E Flat Major Op. 9, No. 2 — Chopin
Mazurka in B Flat Op. 7, No. 1 — Chopin
Saudades do Brazil — Milhaud

Prelude and Fugue in C Sharp Major vol. 1, W.T.C. — J. S. Bach
Kinderscenen Op. 15 — Schumann
Etudes Concert No. 3 in D Flat (Un Sospiro) — Liszt
Intermezzo in E Flat Op. 119, No. 4 — Brahms
Polonaise in A Major Op. 4, No. 1 — Chopin
Jardins sous la pluie — Debussy

*Arranged in program groups representing different centuries, styles, and composers.

Prelude and Fugue in E Major, vol. 2, W.T.C. — J. S. Bach
Album for the Young Op. 68 — Schumann
Ballade in G Minor Op. 23 — Brahms
Hungarian Rhapsody in D Flat No. 6 — Liszt
Tableaux d'une exposition — Moussorgsky-Ravel

Goldberg Variations — J. S. Bach
    Aria with Thirty Transformations
Sonatine — Ravel
Etudes symphoniques — Schumann
Prelude in A Op. 28, No. 7 — Chopin
Prelude in E Minor Op. 28, No. 4 — Chopin

Chromatic Fantasia and Fugue — J. S. Bach
Songs without Words — Mendelssohn
    No. 3 Hunting Song Op. 19, No. 3
       Restlessness Op. 19, No. 5
       Venetian Boat Song
Waltz in C Sharp Minor Op. 64, No. 2 — Chopin
Aufswung Op. 12, No. 2 — Schumann
Concerto in E Flat Op. 75 — Beethoven

Sonata in E Flat Major Op. 78 — Haydn
Impromptu in A Flat Op. 90, No. 4 — Schubert
Moments Musicaux No. 3 in F Minor — Schubert
Scherzo in B Flat Minor — Chopin
Concerto No. 2, Op. 18, in C Minor — Rachmaninoff

Sonata in C Sharp Minor Op. 27, No. 2 (Moonlight) — Beethoven
Variations on a Theme by Haydn Op. 56 — Brahms
Etude in A Flat Op. 25, No. 1 (harp) — Chopin
Reflêts dans l'eau — Debussy
Vòiles — Debussy

Sonata in A Major K331 — Mozart
Variations and Fugue on a Theme by Handel — Brahms
Prelude in C Sharp Minor Op. 3, No. 2 — Rachmaninoff
Nocturne in F sharp Op. 15, No. 2 — Chopin
Cathédrale Engloutie — Debussy
Jeu d'eau — Ravel

Sonata in C Major K545 — Mozart
Etude in E Major Op. 10, No. 3 — Chopin
Etude in C Minor Op. 25, No. 12 — Chopin
Rhapsody in B Minor Op. 79, No. 1 — Brahms
Bird as Prophet — Schumann
Oiseau Tristes — Ravel
Concerto No. 2 in B Flat Minor — Tschaikowsky

Fantasy in D Minor K397 — Mozart
Sonata in D Minor Op. 13 (Pathetique) — Beethoven
Ballade in D Minor Op. 10 — Brahms
Waltz in D Flat Op. 64, No. 1 — Chopin
Three Preludes — Gershwin
The White Peacock — Griffes
Scaramouche — Milhaud

PART IX

Recommended Keyboard Literature for Parallel Study

Collections of Piano Pieces Suitable for Elementary And Intermediate Grades

Bach for Early Grades — compiled from the
Notebook of Anna Magdalene Bach
(Vols. 1, 2, 3)

Boston Music Co.

Bartok, Béla
First Term at the Piano
For Children (Vols. 1, 2)
Mikrokosmos (Vols. 1, 2, 3) (Vols. 4, 5, 6)
Ten Easy Pieces for Piano

Edwin Kalmus
Boosey and Hawkes
Boosey and Hawkes
Boosey and Hawkes

Beringer, Oscar
School of Easy Classics (Augener's Ed.)
Bach (Bk. 1, 2); Handel;
Haydn; Mozart; Beethoven;
Schumann; Schubert; Mendelssohn;
Chopin; Scarlatti; Old English
and French Masters

distributed by Galaxy Corp.

Casella, A.
Eleven Children's Pieces

Associated Music Publ.

Classical Album of Original Piano Pieces

Boston Music Co.

Clark, Frances
Frances Clark Library for Piano Students
Contemporary Piano Literature
(Bks. 1, 2, 3, 4)

Summy-Birchard Publ. Co.

Piano Literature Bk. 1 (An Introduction
   Through Folk Songs and
   Singing Games)
Piano Literature of the 17th, 18th, 19th
   Centuries (Bks. 2, 3, 4)

Diller, Angela — Quaile, Elizabeth   G. Schirmer, Inc.
   Solo Books 1, 2, 3, 4

Easy Classics You Like for the Piano   Clayton F. Summy Co.

Frost, Bernice
   The Adult at the Piano (Vols. 1, 2, 3)   Boston Music Co.

Gretchaninoff, A.
   Children's Book   Opus 98   Edward B. Marks Music Corp.
   Glass Beads   Opus 123   Edwin Kalmus

Hughes, Edwin
   Master Series for the Young   G. Schirmer, Inc.
      Bach, Vol. 1; Handel, Vol. 2;
      Haydn, Vol. 3; Mozart, Vol. 4;
      Beethoven, Vol. 5; Schubert, Vol. 6;
      Weber, Vol. 7; Mendelssohn, Vol. 8;
      Schumann, Vol. 9; Chopin, Vol. 10;
      Grieg, Vol. 11; Tschaikowsky, Vol. 12

Kabalevsky, Dmitri
   Ten Children's Pieces Opus 27 (Bk. 2)   Leeds Music Corp.
   Fifteen Children's Pieces Opus 27 (Bk. 1)

Milhaud, Darius
   The Household Muse   Elkan-Vogel
   L'Enfant Aime   Leeds Music Corp.

Mirovitch, Alfred
   Command of the Keyboard (Vols. 1, 2, 3)   Theodore Presser Co.
   Introduction to the Romantics   G. Schirmer, Inc.

Pinto, Octavio
   Scenas Infantis   G. Schirmer, Inc.
   Children's Festival   G. Schirmer, Inc.

Prokofieff, Serge
   Music for Children   Leeds Music Corp.

Scionti's Road to Piano Artistry   Carl Fischer
   (Vols. 1, 2, 3)

Shostakovich, Dmitri
   Six Children's Pieces for Piano   Leeds Music Corp.

144

Sonatina Album for the Piano	G. Schirmer, Inc.
Sonatinas by Haydn, Clementi, Kuhlau, Beethoven	Clayton F. Summy Co.

Stravinsky, Igor
    The Five Fingers   Mercury Corp. (Omega Music Edition)

Tansman, Alexandre

Children at Play	Leeds Music Corp.
Pour les Enfants (Vols. 1, 2, 3, 4)	Associated Music Publ.
Ten Diversions for the Young Pianist	Associated Music Publ.
Piano in Progress (Vols. 1, 2)	Edward B. Marks Corp.

Toch, Ernst
    Echoes from a Small Town   Associated Music Publ.

Tschaikovsky, Peter I.
    Album for the Young   Opus 39   Edward B. Marks Music Corp.

Tureck, Roselyn
    Introduction to the Performance of Bach   Oxford University Press

PART X

A Study Guide

A Plan for Four Terms

This guide tells in what order to study the materials in this book. Although it is planned for four terms, it can be completed in more or less time depending on the age and ability of the student and on the amount of time spent on it.

In the parts devoted to scales, arpeggios, keyboard exercises, and technical exercises, it is expected that the student will continue to review things from the previous terms which help his technique and which increase his understanding of the keyboard.

Scales and Arpeggios

First Term

1. All major and minor (natural, harmonic, melodic) scales, using traditional fingering, ascending and descending, one octave, each hand alone.
2. All tonic arpeggios one octave, each hand alone.

Second Term

1. All major and minor (natural, harmonic, melodic) scales, using traditional fingering, ascending and descending, two octaves, hands together.
2. All tonic arpeggios, major and minor, two octaves, first, each hand alone, then hands together.
3. Chromatic, whole tone, pentatonic, modal scales played in their simplest form demonstrating a knowledge of each.

Third Term

1. All major and minor scales, played in rhythms of two (♩) — two octaves, three (♩) — three octaves, four (♩♩♩♩) — four octaves.
2. All tonic arpeggios, major and minor, played in rhythms like scales (see 1.)
3. Dominant seventh arpeggios, two octaves each hand alone; then hands together.
4. Improvisation on the whole tone and pentatonic scales (see part on pedalling for ideas).
5. Chromatic scale as a technical exercise to develop speed and clarity.

Fourth Term

1. All major and minor scales harmonized in four part harmony.
2. All tonic and dominant seventh arpeggios, in all positions, in rhythms, two, three, four octaves, hands together.
3. Modal scales, reviewed untransposed, then transposed.
4. Improvisation on the modal scales.
5. Improvisation on the tonic and dominant seventh arpeggios.

Formal Keyboard Harmony Exercises

First Term

1. Intervals
2. Triads
3. Locate and play I, IV, V triads in all keys.
4. Inversions of all major and minor triads.
5. The following chord progressions in a three part bass clef pattern (three positions) all keys:

    I IV I, i iv i
    I   V I, i   V i
    I IV I V I, i iv i V i

6. Inversions of all V7 chords
7. I IV I V7 I, i iv i V7 i in a three part bass clef pattern (three positions).
8. Improvisation on all chord progressions (waltz and march bass, etc.)

Second Term

1. Diatonic chords in every key
   a— each hand alone
   b— hands together
2. The following chord progressions in four part harmony, all keys:

   I IV I, i iv i
   I V I, i V i
   I IV V I, i iv V i
   I V7 I, i V7 i
   I IV V7 I, i iv V7 i

3. Improvisation on all chord progressions
   a— melody and accompaniment style
   b— hymn and chorale style

Third Term

1. The following progressions in every key (two positions, four part harmony)

   I ii6 I$_4^6$ V I, i ii6 i$_4^6$ V i

2. Neopolitan Sixth in a cadence (every minor key)

   i ii$_{3b}^{6b}$ i$_4^6$ V7 i and i ii$_{3b}^{6b}$ V7 i

3. Improvisations on the foregoing progressions.
4. Diatonic secondary sevenths and their resolutions (major mode).
5. Dominant chords: V, V7, V^{9b}, V^{11}, V^{11}#, V^{13}, V$_{9b}^{13b}$

Fourth Term

1. Secondary dominants (major mode) in three and four part forms.
2. Modulations by means of the dominant to:
   the dominant key
   the super-tonic key
   the sub-mediant key
   sub-dominant key
   mediant key

3. Improvisation on chord progressions to other keys.

Informal Harmonization and Transposition of Melodies

First Term

1. Melodies harmonized with I and V (or V7), and i and V (or V7)
2. Melodies harmonized with I, IV and V (or V7), and with I, iv and v (or V7)
3. The foregoing melodies transposed into every key.

Second Term

1. Melodies to be harmonized I IV V7, i iv V7, or I IV and an inversion of the dominant seventh chord.
2. The foregoing melodies transposed into every key.

Third Term

1. Selected melodies harmonized with I ii6 I$^6_4$ V I or with other progressions studied this far.

Fourth Term

1. Melodies using secondary dominants
2. The foregoing melodies transposed into other keys.

Basic Exercises for the Development of Coordination and Technique

First Term

1. A look inside the piano to see how it works.
2. A study of the three pedals and their functions
   a— pedal exercises
3. Exercises to improve fingering, proper phrasing, legato and staccato touch, even tempo
   a— Applied in pieces being studied

Second Term

1. Exercises to improve fingering, proper phrasing, legato and staccato touch, even tempo
2. Applied in pieces being studied.

Third Term

1. Exercises to improve independence of fingers, smooth moving under of the thumb, accuracy of attack.
2. Review of technique of second term.
3. Applied in pieces being studied.

Fourth Term

1. Exercises for speed and facility, changing fingers while holding down notes, playing contrapuntally, playing repeated notes accurately and evenly, accuracy in playing sequences of chord progressions.
2. Applied in pieces being studied.

Piano Adaptations of Instrumental and Vocal Music

First Term

1. *Symphony No. 9 in D Minor* Op. 125 (1824) — Beethoven
2. *The Creation* — Haydn
3. *My Heart Ever Faithful* from Cantata No. 68 — Bach

Second Term

1. *Don Giovanni* — Mozart
2. *Symphony in D Minor* — Franck

150

3. *Symphony No. 8 (Unfinished)* — Schubert
4. *Variations on a Theme by Haydn* Op. 56 — Brahms
5. *Hänsel and Gretel* — Humperdinck

Third Term

1. *The Messiah* — Handel
2. *Chorale No. 42* — Bach
3. *Symphony No. 1 (Clock)* — Haydn
4. *Symphony No. 40* — Mozart

Fourth Term

1. Chorale No. 54 (partial realizations) — Bach
2. *Till Eulenspiegel* Op. 28 — R. Strauss
3. *Die Meistersinger* — Wagner
4. *L'Arlésienne Suite No. 1 and No. 2* — Bizet

Songs to Play and Sing

Second Term

1. America
2. America, the Beautiful
3. Home on the Range
4. O Come, All Ye Faithful

Third Term

1. We Gather Together
2. Drink to Me Only With Thine Eyes
3. Swing Low Sweet Chariot

Fourth Term

1. The Ash Grove
2. Greensleeves
3. When Johnny Comes Marching Home
4. The Star-Spangled Banner

Standard Piano Compositions for Listening

The programs listed here are to be used to familiarize the elementary piano student with famous piano concert compositions. A free choice can be made depending on the recordings available, the concerts being given in the area, and the tastes of the student.

DATE DUE

MAY 2 6 1975			
SEP 1 8 79			
FEB 2 0 1986			